T H E

Splicing

H A N D B O O K

THE
Splicing
HANDBOOK

Techniques for Modern and Traditional Ropes

BARBARA MERRY
with JOHN DARWIN

**INTERNATIONAL MARINE
PUBLISHING COMPANY
Camden, Maine 04843**

Published by International Marine Publishing Company

10   9   8   7   6   5   4   3   2

Library of Congress Cataloging in Publication Data

Merry, Barbara.
   The splicing handbook.

   1. Knots and splices.   I. Title
VM533.M47   1987   623.88'82   87-22537

ISBN 0-87742-952-9

International Marine Publishing Company offers software for
sale. For information and a catalog, please contact TAB
Software Department, Blue Ridge Summit, PA 17294-9850.

Questions regarding the content of this book should be
addressed to:

International Marine Publishing Company
Division of TAB Books, Inc.
P.O. Box 220
Camden, ME 04843

Typeset by Typeworks, Belfast, ME
Printed and bound by BookCrafters, Chelsea, MI
Design by Lurelle Cheverie
Illustrated by Ben Martinez
Additional illustrations by Rod McCormick
Illustration on page 10 by Rob Shetterly
Production by Janet Robbins

To my daughter,
Shannon, with love.

Acknowledgments

My thanks to Jonathan Eaton and
Barbara Hatch, my editors at International Marine,
for their help and enthusiasm.

Contents

CONTENTS

1

Introduction to Splicing

Rope in use is attached to something else—to another rope, to an object to be moved or prevented from moving, or to an object that prevents the rope from moving. The attachment can be accomplished with a knot, but knots are bulky and by their nature cut the breaking strength of rope in half. The alternative is a splice, which is capable of attaining a rope's full strength.

Splicing teaches you not only about the splice itself, but also about the construction and quality of the raw material. The knowledge gained from practicing the splices in this handbook should enable you to splice *any* general-purpose rope.

No single splicing technique can work on all rope because the constructions vary considerably. Rope designers, who are functional artists much like architects, seek a perfect construction using the characteristics of various fibers: strengths, abrasion-resistance, weight, and elasticity. They must consider resistance to heat, cold, sunlight, chemicals, water, dye, and microorganisms, as well as construction possibilities such as braiding, twisting, knitting, plaiting, wrapping, and gluing.

High-Tech Rope Construction

Egyptians on the Mediterranean worked with twisted and braided ropes 3,000 years ago, and seamen 12,000 miles away in the Far East did also. Their ropes, knots, and splices were much like those we use today, except that ropes of strong synthetic fibers have all but replaced natural fibers over the past few decades. With increased international shipping, ropes from all over the world are now evident in large commercial harbors.

Any rope is a bundle of textile fibers combined in a usable form. For example, a ½-inch-diameter nylon rope might have 90,000 tiny fibers, each with a tensile strength of 2 ounces, giving it a potential breaking strength of 11,000 pounds if the fibers could all be pulled in such a way that each achieved its maximum strength. The 90,000 fibers can be bonded, twisted, or braided, or these construction techniques can be combined to make a working rope. The federal government usually requires a minimum breaking strength for general use of only 5,800 pounds for ½-inch 3-strand nylon rope; in nylon double-braid rope, a strength of 15 percent more is specified. The difference between the nylon's potential strength of 11,000 pounds and the actual strength is due to the shearing action on the twisted fibers when the rope is loaded to its ultimate strength.

The old standby, 3-strand twisted rope, is the most economical rope available today at about 30 cents a foot for ½-inch diameter. It consists of fibers (often nylon) spun into yarns, which are then formed into the strands. Three-strand is commonly used for anchor rodes and mooring and docking lines.

Double-braid rope came into common use when it was discovered that careful design and construction could induce a braided hollow core to share the load equally with its braided cover. When you work with this rope, you must preserve the original coat-to-core spatial relationship to retain its inherent strength, so tie the Slip Knot, called for in the splice directions for this construction, both properly and tightly.

Dacron double braid is generally stronger than 3-strand twisted nylon rope, but it is also more costly at about 55 cents per foot, and the

2

difference in cost should be considered against the line's intended use. Whenever the breaking strength of rope is critical, the manufacturer's specifications should be consulted. Some low-cost rope on the market is made to look like double-braid, but it is not, so check the product carefully and deal with reputable suppliers.

Polyester double-braid rope is low stretch and resists kinking and hockling; it is especially good for halyards and sheets.

Braid with 3-strand core is a common line for running rigging on yachts. As its name implies, the outer cover is braided, with 16 plaits, or braids. The core, a 3-strand twist, carries most of the strength. Often called Marlow, for its English manufacturer, it is sold with standard and fuzzy covers, the latter being soft on the hands and holding knots well. The covers are available in colors, a convenience, for example, when one must find a halyard quickly in a maze of running rigging. Marlow can be difficult to find in some areas.

Braid with parallel core is another rope with most of the strength in the core. It stretches very little, and pound-for-pound, it is as strong as stainless steel wire (see chart), so there is a trend toward using it to replace wire on recreational nonracing sailboats. This rope is also stiff and a poor choice where bend and flex are important, such as when a line must pass through a block.

Hollow-braid rope of polypropylene floats and is most often used for waterskiing tow lines and around life rings.

Nylon 8-plait rope, also called square braid, is a common rope on commercial vessels. It consists of four strand pairs, one member of

Wire Halyard Replacement Chart

7 x 19 Stainless Wire (inches)	Braid with Parallel Core Sta-Set X (inches)	Double Braid Samson XLS 900 (inches)
1/8	5/16	3/16
5/32	3/8	1/4
3/16	7/16	5/16
7/32	1/2	5/16
1/4	9/16	3/8

This chart is for general comparison only. Follow the manufacturer's specific recommendations for all working loads.

each pair having right-laid yarns and the other having left-laid yarns. (To determine the direction of lay, consider the rope with its end pointing away from you. Right lay spirals up and to the right.)

More rounded than 8-plait, 12-plait rope is used most often for towing hawsers. The plaited ropes are easy to inspect for damage and can be dropped in a heap on deck without hockling.

Inexpensive rope such as clothesline, often sold precoiled in hardware stores, is not suitable for marine use.

Synthetic Rope Materials

Both the materials and the construction of synthetic ropes mandate splicing techniques that were never needed with natural fibers. For example, manila, a natural fiber, holds its shape after it has been unlaid, but nylon changes shape very quickly as the strands slip away from each other and divide into yarns. The splicer must adapt to this tendency by sealing the rope ends as described in the splicing section of this book.

Synthetics present a range of characteristics (see chart). Manila,

General Characteristics of Synthetic Marine Rope Materials

	Nylon	Polyester (Dacron)	Polypropylene	Aramid (Kevlar)
Strength	strong	strong	strong	very strong
Stretch	stretches	low-stretch	low-stretch	low-stretch
Shrinkage	shrinks	low-shrink	low-shrink	no shrink
Flotation	sinks	sinks	floats	sinks
Cost	moderate	moderate	cheap	high
Common Uses	mooring and docking lines	sheets and halyards	water ski towlines	running rigging

once used almost exclusively, is now favored mainly by traditionalists. It is heavy for its strength—twice the weight of nylon—and rots from the inside, a problem that is difficult to detect.

Polypropylene is the lightest synthetic rope now in production. Its great advantage is its ability to float on fresh and salt water. It has a low melting point and should not be used near heat-producing mechanical devices. It also has a low resistance to sunlight.

Ropes made of nylon are strong, but stretch significantly. They have excellent resistance to sunlight, common alkalies, and acids. Polyester (Dacron and Terylene) is a low-stretch rope with a low tensile strength. Both nylon and polyester are sold in spun and filament form. The spun rope is usually fuzzy and is made of fibers 4 to 10 inches long; the continuous-filament rope has a shiny surface and is stronger and heavier.

Quick Guide to Strength of Rope Materials

Diameter in Inches of 3-Strand or Double-Braid Nylon Rope

	¹⁄₁₆	⅛	³⁄₁₆	¼	⁵⁄₁₆	⅜	⁷⁄₁₆	½	⅝	¾	⅞	1
DIAMETER IN MILLIMETERS	1.5	3	5	6	8	9	11	13	16	19	22	25
BRAID SIZE	2	4	6	8	10	12	14	16	20	24	28	32
CIRCUMFERENCE IN INCHES	³⁄₁₆	⅜	⅝	¾	1	1⅛	1¼	1½	2	2¼	2¾	3
WEIGHT IN FEET PER POUND	400	200	100	65	40	30	20	16	10	7	5	4
BREAKING STRENGTH IN POUNDS	200	400	750	1,000	2,000	3,000	4,000	6,000	10,000	17,000	20,000	25,000

Polypropylene – 20 percent lighter in weight than nylon; 20 percent weaker
Polyester – 20 percent heavier than nylon; about same strength
Aramid (Kevlar) – 40 percent heavier than nylon; 200 percent stronger

Note: This chart is for 3-strand and double-braid rope of the same weight and quality. The safe working load of rope is about 10 percent of its breaking strength. In *ALL* critical situations, consult the manufacturer's load recommendations.

Kevlar, DuPont's aramid fiber, is combined with Dacron for extra strength in some double-braid ropes.

Combination rope is any rope constructed of more than one synthetic fiber. Most common on fishing boats is 3-strand twisted polyester and polypropylene, which has the general characteristics of 100% polyester, but is cheaper.

Small Stuff

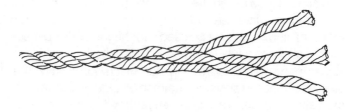

Small stuff is generally considered to be ³⁄₁₆- to ½-inch diameter rope, 3-strand twisted. Constructed of firm, spliceable manila or nylon, it is favored by the boatowner for light-duty use and decorative projects.

Definitions within the rope industry differ, however, and some also group the following with small stuff:

• **Twine.** Twine doesn't look like rope, although it is composed of fibers. It is usually less than ³⁄₁₆ inch in diameter. Waxed whipping twine is constructed of nylon or polyester and coated with wax to make whipping and seizing easier. The wax also protects against weathering.

• **Marline.** Marline comprises two strands of hemp, left laid, and is coated with tar to protect against weathering, giving it a characteristic burned odor. It can be used for lashing or seizing.

• **Clothesline, sash cord, mason line,** and **braided utility line.** These usually have a solid core and are not spliceable.

Rope Care

It's foolish to buy good rope and then treat it carelessly, because rope that is damaged will have a reduced breaking strength and a shorter life. Here are some ways to preserve the lifespan of your rope:

• To take rope off a storage reel properly, avoiding kinks, twists, or hockles in the line, let the reel rotate freely around a horizontal pipe suspended or supported at both ends.

• Store rope in a clean dry area, off the floor, out of sunlight, and away from acid fumes.

• Keep rope from chafing against standing rigging and rough surfaces. Be wary of rusty or sharp chocks, bitts, and winches that will abrade the rope. Pulleys and blocks should be correctly sized and should turn freely.

• If rope is chafed or frayed, cut out the damaged portion and splice. A good splice is safer than a damaged section.

• It is not generally necessary to oil or lubricate rope; if you do, use a product that is specifically designed for that purpose.

• Use whipping, tape, or an end splice on the bitter end of rope to prevent unlaying.

• Check rope often for deterioration, opening the lay of 3-strand and plaited rope for inspection.

• If rope is dragged over the ground, rocks and dirt can be picked up. Eventually these particles can work into the rope, cutting the fibers.

• The proper way to dry a line is to lay it up on a grating in long fakes to allow good air circulation, thus preventing mildew and rot.

• Do not hesitate to wash synthetic rope by hand. Coil and tie it loosely, wash with a mild soap, then lay it out to dry.

• Don't use a rope in a situation where strength is critical if the rope has ever been subjected to a sudden, heavy load.

• A smooth taper will result in a more efficient splice.

Splicing Tools

It is part of the splicing tradition to use tools that aid in separating the strands of rope. Just as high-tech rope and synthetic materials require new splicing techniques, they also mandate specialized tools to facilitate those procedures.

The Swedish fid is used for 3-strand, 8-plait, and 12-plait rope. The pointed end separates tightly twisted strands, and the concave blade guides individual strands into position. A Swedish fid also pulls soft ropes into place for strand insertion by exerting an even pull so there is less distortion. It is easiest to work with a fid that is in proportion to the diameter of the rope, but any fid that is not too small to guide the rope will do. Swedish fids increase in circumference with length, and are available in lengths of 6 inches for about $4.50, 12 inches for $6.50, and 14 inches for $7.50.

Tubular fids aid in splicing double-braid rope, which consists of a hollow braided core surrounded by a braided cover. When the core is removed from the cover during splicing, the cover also becomes a hollow tube. The tubular fid, also called a hollow fid, guides the rope through these passageways as the splice is worked.

The fid has a pointed end to ease movement through the rope and an indented end where the working end of the rope is inserted. It is important that this be a snug fit, so the fids are made in sizes corresponding to standard rope diameters. If you have on hand a fid that is only slightly too large, the rope can be held in place with tape.

Measurements taken on the rope during splicing commonly use portions of the appropriate fid's length as units. A full fid length is the entire length of the fid; short and long fid lengths are marked on the

Approximate Lengths of Fid
Sections in Inches

Rope Diameter	Short	Long	Full
1/4″	2	3½	5½
5/16″	2½	4¼	6¾
3/8″	3	4¾	7¾
7/16″	3½	6	9½
1/2″	4	7	11
9/16″	4¼	8	12¼
5/8″	4½	9½	14

fid. (See the chart for the approximate lengths of these fid sections in inches.) Tubular fids range in price from about $4.25 for the ¼-inch diameter to $6.00 for ⅝-inch.

A special splicing tool sold by Marlow Ropes, manufacturer of braid with 3-strand core, is necessary to splice that rope. The tool is usually available where the rope is sold and consists of a small-diameter wire with a hook at one end and an eye at the other. The hook is used as a handle, and the eye, threaded with one or more of the core strands, is pulled behind.

A Uni-Fid, manufactured by New England Ropes of New Bedford, Massachusetts, is needed to splice braid with parallel core. This rope has a core of parallel fibers wrapped in a gauze-like material, all within a braided cover. The tool consists of a small-diameter wire with a hook smaller than that on the Marlow splicing tool. A pointed end on the Uni-Fid is pushed through the rope, while the hook, which has been inserted through the gauze, follows behind.

The Uni-Fid, like the tubular fid, is divided into fid lengths, and the chart comparing fid lengths to inches applies equally to it.

Not all splicing tools are used to manipulate rope during the working of a splice. The thimble is such a tool; it is a teardrop-shaped metal support for an Eye Splice, with a grooved outer edge for the rope.

Variations of the Eye Splice are found in chapter after chapter of this handbook, showing its popularity and virtuosity despite differences in rope construction and materials. Without a thimble, it is effective for light-duty use, such as on a topping lift or dinghy painter. With a thimble, the Eye Splice is ready for heavy use, when wear and chafe must be considered. A thimble should be used whenever the line will be attached to chain, swivels, or shackles, such as on the anchor end of an anchor rode.

Thimbles are available in only one eye size for any given diameter of rope. If a larger eye is needed for light-duty use and some protection is desired, a rubber hose can be placed over the crown of the eye to substitute for a thimble.

3-Strand Twisted Rope

Technique is important to preserve splice strength, even with basic 3-strand rope, which is sold in sizes ranging from ⅛ inch to 2 inches in diameter.

Eye Splice

This is the most common splice.
Take care that the tucks lie
neatly, because much
of the rope strength can be lost
if the strands are twisted incorrectly.

TOOLS AND MATERIALS

3-Strand twisted rope
Swedish fid
Vinyl tape or whipping twine
Scissors or sharp knife
Hot knife or heat source
Ruler
Thimble (optional)

Unlay (untwist) the rope for 2 or 3 inches and tape each of the three individual ends or seize them tightly with twine (see Chapter 11). Tape again at the point where the unlaying should end. For this splice in ¾-inch rope, that would be about 12 inches from the working end. Add the amount of rope necessary to form the eye, or loop. Tape again. This spot is called the throat of the splice.

Unlay back to the first piece of tape. To avoid a twist in the eye of the finished splice, untwist the rope just half a turn between the pieces of tape.

To do the first tuck, raise a strand just below the tape on the standing part of the rope and insert the middle working strand under it. You can usually do this with your fingers, but if the rope is twisted too tightly, use a Swedish fid (see page 8). Insert this splicing tool under the strand, and then place the middle working strand through the fid. Pull the strand into place and remove the tool.

The first time you work this splice, place a single hash mark on the strand that you just tucked. Numbering the working strands should help you to keep track of the tucking process.

Tuck the next working strand over the strand you just tucked under, and under the strand just below it. Mark this with two hash marks.

Turn the entire piece over. You have one working strand left to tuck, and there is one strand left in the standing part of the rope that doesn't have a working strand under it. Make this tuck, continuing to work counter to the lay, or twist, of the rope (left to right in the drawings). Mark with three hash marks.

The first round of tucks is now complete. Tighten if necessary by pulling on the strand ends.

Take care when you tuck that you use all three strands in each round and that you tuck under a strand in the standing part of the rope and not under one of your working strands.

Make two more rounds of tucks unless the rope is nylon, which holds better with five or six rounds.

For a smooth, better-looking splice, finish with the California method: After the rounds of tucks are complete, the first strand is left as is. The next strand is tucked once (as in the beginning steps), and the last strand is tucked twice.

Cut the ends off close, seal or melt the ends of synthetic rope with a hot knife or match, and remove the tape.

Decorative Eye Splice

The decorative knot set at the neck of
this dressed-up version of the Eye
Splice does not affect its strength, but
you should position the knot to
avoid chafing when the splice is in use.

TOOLS AND MATERIALS

3-Strand twisted rope
Swedish fid
Vinyl tape or whipping twine
Scissors or sharp knife
Hot knife or heat source
Ruler

Unlay (untwist) the rope for 2 or 3 inches, and tape each of the individual ends or seize them tightly with twine (see Chapter 11). Tape again at the point where the unlaying should end. For this splice in ¾-inch rope, that would be 24 inches from the working end of the rope. Add the amount of rope necessary to form the eye and tape again at the throat of the splice.

Unlay the rope back to the first piece of tape. To avoid a twist in the eye of the finished splice, untwist the rope just half a turn between the pieces of tape.

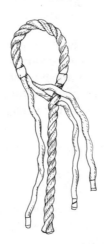

To do the first tuck, raise a strand just below the tape on the standing part of the rope and insert the middle working strand under it. You can usually do this with your fingers, but if the line is twisted too tightly, use a Swedish fid.

16

Tuck the next working strand over the strand you just tucked under, and under the strand just below it.

Turn the entire piece over. You have one working strand left to tuck, and there is one strand left in the standing part of the rope that doesn't have a working strand under it. Make this tuck, continuing to work counter to the lay of the rope (left to right in the drawings).

The first round of tucks is now complete; tighten by pulling on the strand ends.

Take care when you tuck that you use all three strands in each round and that you tuck under a strand in the standing part of the rope and not under one of your working strands. To this point, the procedure is identical to that for the basic Eye Splice.

Now tie a Double Wall and Crown Knot as follows. Hold the throat of the splice between your thumb and forefinger with the strands emerging upward and spreading over the top of your fist like the petals of a flower. To begin the Wall Knot, the first step in this three-step knot, take any strand, and moving counterclockwise, lead it under the strand next to it. (We will call this the second strand.) Allow the bight (loop) formed to remain prominent because you will need it later.

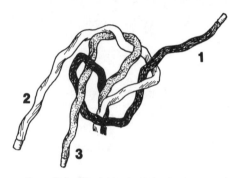

The second strand leads under the first strand, then under the third strand, as in the drawing. The third strand then leads under the second strand and up through the bight formed in the first step. This sounds complicated, but if you follow the illustration as you work, you'll see it is straightforward.

Gather the knot in evenly, but keep it loose.

The Crown Knot is the reverse of the Wall Knot. Take any strand, and continuing to work counterclockwise, lead it over the strand next to it, leaving a bight. Lead the second strand over the first strand, then over the third strand. Lead the third strand over the second strand and down through the bight.

The third and final step doubles the entire knot; this is the simplest part of the entire process. Beginning with any strand, duplicate its journey through the knot by eyeballing, poking, and wiggling it. (You left the knot loose in anticipation of this step.)

The strand's journey began near the point where its end now emerges; guide the end back into the knot at that point and retrace the circuit, in effect doubling the strand. Take care as you work that you

don't separate other parallel pairs. It's so easy once you get rolling that you have only to stop yourself from going too far. If the strand starts to appear in triplicate, you need to back up a little. Repeat this process for all three strands, and you'll have doubled the knot. Now cinch the strands firmly and evenly.

For a smooth, better-looking splice, finish with the California method: After three full rounds of tucks (five with nylon rope), the first strand is left as is. The next strand is tucked once (as in the beginning steps), and the last strand is tucked twice.

Cut the ends off close, seal or melt the ends of synthetic rope with a hot knife or match, and remove the tape.

Ring Splice

This splice attaches the working end
of a rope to a ring or clew.
Chafing between the ring and strands
is minimal if the first round of
tucks is pulled tight. Many sailors
and fishermen use it to attach rope to
chain, but directions for a safer,
more professional Rope-to-Chain Splice
are given in Chapter 9.

TOOLS AND MATERIALS

3-Strand twisted rope
Swedish fid
Ring
Vinyl tape or whipping twine
Scissors or sharp knife
Hot knife or heat source
Ruler

Unlay the rope 2 or 3 inches and tape or seize each of the individual strands. Tape where the unlaying is to end. For ¾-inch rope, that would be 12 inches from the working end for a three-tuck splice. Unlay the rope to the tape.

Pass the first strand on the left (A) through the ring from front to back and around the ring coming out to the right of itself. Work strands B and C the same way, then pass strand C to the left, over itself, and back between itself and strand B. Draw up this round of tucks tightly and remove the tape.

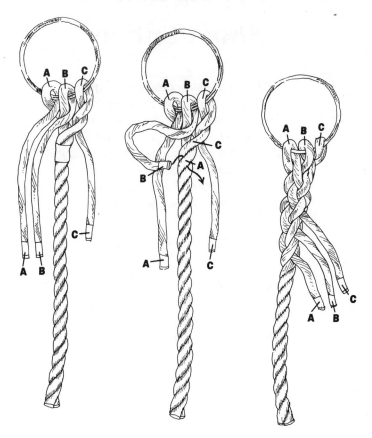

To work the second round of tucks, pick up the middle strand (B), pass it over the base of the third strand (C) and tuck it under the strand below (A).

Pick up the working end of strand A, pass it over strand B and under the strand below. It will come out where B tucked in on this second round.

Turn the work over and finish the round with strand C passing over strand A and under the strand below.

For a smooth, better-looking splice, finish with the California method: After three full rounds of tucks (five with nylon rope), the first strand is left as is. The next strand is tucked once, and the last strand is tucked twice.

Cut the ends off close, seal or melt the ends of synthetic rope with a hot knife or match, and remove the tape.

Short Splice

This is the strongest splice for
putting two lengths of twisted rope together.
The rope thickens at the splice, so it
should not be used when a line must
pass over an exact-sized pulley or through
an opening only slightly larger than
itself. In these situations, it is
better to use a whole length of rope.

TOOLS AND MATERIALS

3-Strand twisted rope (two pieces)
Swedish fid
Vinyl tape or whipping twine
Scissors or sharp knife
Hot knife or heat source
Ruler

Unlay one end of each rope for 2 or 3 inches and tape or seize the six individual ends. Continue unlaying: for ¾-inch rope, 12 inches in each rope is ample for a three-tuck splice. Tape to prevent the ropes from unlaying farther.

Interlace, or marry, the two pieces of rope so that each strand is parallel to the corresponding strand of the other piece. To hold the splice together, place a temporary seizing of tape or twine where the two pieces join.

The first tuck of the round is started by placing one strand over the standing part of its corresponding strand and under the next. This can, in most cases, be done with your fingers, but if the rope is twisted too tightly, use the Swedish fid to smooth the way.

Rotate the work and repeat until all three strands are tucked. One round of tucks is now complete; finish the other side of the seizing in the same way.

Remove the seizing and tighten the splice by pulling on the strand ends.

Repeat all the tucks two more times. For nylon rope, continue for a total of five or six rounds.

For a smooth, better-looking splice, finish with the California method: After three full rounds of tucks, the first strand is left as is. The next strand is tucked once, and the last strand is tucked twice.

Cut the ends off close, seal or melt the ends of synthetic rope with a hot knife or match, and remove the tape.

End Splice

**The bitter end of a rope often is finished
with whipping; this splice is a good
alternative when improved grip is important.**

TOOLS AND MATERIALS

3-Strand twisted rope
Swedish fid
Vinyl tape or whipping twine
Scissors or sharp knife
Hot knife or heat source
Ruler

Unlay about 3 inches of rope and tape or seize the individual ends. Then tape where the unlaying should end. For this splice in ¾-inch rope, that would be about 12 inches from the working end. Unlay the rope to the tape.

Hold the rope at the tape between your thumb and forefinger with the strands emerging upward and spreading over the top of your fist like the petals of a flower.

To begin, crown the three strands. To do this, take any strand, and moving counterclockwise, lead it over the strand next to it. (We will call this the second strand.) Allow the resultant bight, or loop, to remain prominent, because you will need it later.

The second strand leads over the first strand, then over the third strand. This third strand then leads over the second strand and down through the bight formed in your first step. The crown is now complete; draw it up tightly.

Remove the tape or seizing. For the first round of tucks, raise a strand on the standing part of the line and insert any adjacent working strand under it. You can usually do this with your fingers, but if the rope is twisted too tightly, use a Swedish fid.

Tuck a working end over the strand you just tucked under, and under the strand just below it.

Turn the entire piece over. You have one working strand left to tuck,

and there is one strand left in the standing part of the rope that doesn't have a working strand under it. Make this tuck, continuing to work counter to the lay of the rope.

The first round of tucks is now complete. Tighten if necessary by pulling on the strand ends.

Repeat the series of tucks two more times, unless the rope is nylon, which holds better with five or six rounds.

For a smooth, better-looking splice, finish with the California method: After the rounds of tucks are complete, the first strand is left as is. The next strand is tucked once (as in the beginning steps), and the last strand is tucked twice.

Cut the ends off close, seal or melt the ends of synthetic rope with a hot knife or match, and remove the tape.

3-Strand Splicing Projects

These splicing projects are fun as well as practical, but shop carefully for your rope so you don't work for hours and then end up with a frazzled mess. If necessary, spend a few cents more for good quality, 3-strand twisted rope or small stuff.

Use ¼-inch nylon or spun Dacron for the key lanyard, leash, and collar; use manila or combination rope for the railing. Ask the salesperson to unlay a short portion of the rope after heat-sealing or taping the three strands and check to see that each strand holds its individual twist. If the yarns fly apart, or if the rope does not retain its shape, search for better rope. Remember to ask the salesperson to tape the rope to keep it from unlaying farther on your trip home.

Key Lanyard

A simple, attractive lanyard to hold keys or a knife

TOOLS AND MATERIALS

3-Strand small stuff
    26 inches of ³⁄₁₆-inch or ¼-inch rope
Ring
Vinyl tape or whipping twine
Scissors or sharp knife
Ruler

A 26-inch piece of small stuff, or cordage (rope less than ½ inch in diameter), will give you a finished lanyard length of about 12 inches. Attach the ring using the Ring Splice with at least five tucks; allow 6 inches for the splice. On the other end, form the loop, allowing 8 inches for the Decorative Eye Splice with five tucks.

Directions for the Ring Splice and Decorative Eye Splice are given in Chapter 2.

Dog Collar and Leash

A classy but inexpensive set for your dog

TOOLS AND MATERIALS

3-Strand twisted rope
1 or 2 Rings
Spring tension clip
Vinyl tape or whipping twine
Scissors or sharp knife
Ruler

For a collar of ½-inch rope, allow enough to comfortably encircle the dog's neck, plus 12 inches for the splices.

For a loose collar, attach both ends of the collar to the same ring using Ring Splices. For a choke-style training collar, use a Ring Splice to attach a ring to each end of the collar.

Allow 5½ feet of rope for a 4-foot leash. Attach the clip to one end using a Ring Splice. Finish the other end with an Eye Splice, making the eye large enough for your hand.

Directions for the Ring Splice and Eye Splice are given in Chapter 2.

Rope Railings with Wall and Crown Knot

This is an unusually pretty way to frame a favorite area in the garden or to line a walkway. It can also be used as an inexpensive safety railing around docks and piers. The Double Wall and Crown Knot serves as a stop-knot where the rope passes through a post.

TOOLS AND MATERIALS

3-Strand twisted rope
Vinyl tape or whipping twine
Scissors or sharp knife
Ruler

For directions on tying the Wall and Crown Knot, see the Decorative Eye Splice in Chapter 2.

4

Double-Braid Rope

Double-braid rope is composed of a braided core inside a braided coat, or outer covering; both contribute to the strength of the rope. It is important, therefore, that when your splice is finished, the coat covers the core smoothly and evenly, as it did when manufactured. To accomplish this, be sure to tie a Slip Knot, as directed for each splice, to keep the core from sliding up inside the cover while you work.

The weak spot on spliced rope lies on the standing side of the splice, where the rope is first disturbed. Tapered ends are usually buried there, so follow the tapering directions carefully.

Eye Splice

**Follow these steps to put an eye or
thimble at the end of double-braid rope.**

TOOLS AND MATERIALS

Double-braid rope
Tubular fid
Vinyl tape
Scissors or sharp knife
Marking pen
Waxed whipping twine
Needle
Thimble (optional)

Trim the end of the rope evenly, cutting off melted ends, or tape the end to be spliced. Using a tubular fid (see page 8), measure one full fid length from the tape and label this reference point with an R. (To determine the appropriate fid for the rope you are using, see page 8.)

Add the amount of rope necessary to form the eye or the loop around the thimble (see page 10), if one is used. Mark an X there, at the throat of the splice. This is a complicated splice to complete with a thimble, so measurements are critical.

Move up the rope at least five full fid lengths and tie a tight Slip Knot.

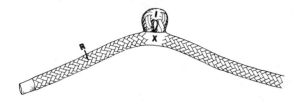

Return to the X and gently push aside the strands of the coat, the rope's outer covering, to expose its inner core. Pull a small loop of the core through the coat as carefully as possible, and draw a single hash

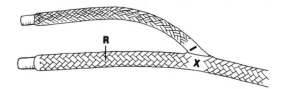

mark across the top of the core. Then continue pulling out the core until its working end is completely exposed, and tape the end. Work the cover down into place to confirm that the X and hash mark are aligned and equal distances from the coat end and core end, respectively.

Now pull out more core, this time from the standing part of the rope, and measure one short fid length from the single hash mark. (Short and long fid lengths are marked on tubular fids; for the measurement in inches, see page 9.) Make two hash marks there.

Continue along the core for one full fid length plus one short fid length, pulling out more from the standing part if necessary. Make three hash marks.

For maximum strength in the splice, you will need to draw the rope's outer coat into its core and then its core into the coat. It will help to remember that the coat is marked with letters, and the core with hash marks.

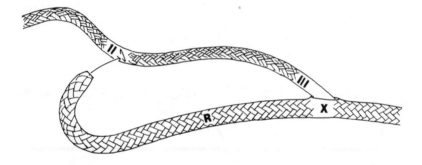

Pinch the taped end of the coat and insert it into the hollow end of the fid, taping it in place. Push the fid into the core at two hash marks and out at three hash marks. Be careful not to twist the coat. Pull until the R comes into view. The core will bunch up as you do so, but this will correct itself later.

To taper the end of the coat, work toward the fid from R, and count off seven sets of pics, or parallel ribs, that run clockwise; mark this spot with a T. Continue toward the fid, marking every seventh pair with a dot so you will know where to cut.

Now go back to the R, this time marking the counterclockwise pics for tapering. To offset the tapering on these pics, mark your first dot at the fourth pair. From there, mark every seventh counterclockwise pair until you reach the fid.

Remove the fid and the tape. Cut and remove a single strand at each marked pic along the coat.

While holding the core, pull the coat until the T shows beyond the two hash marks. Take care not to lose the end of the tapered coat into the core.

For extra strength, the core end should be drawn through the coat, past the throat of the splice and into the standing part of the rope. Measure from X toward the Slip Knot one short half of the tubular fid; label this spot Z.

Tape the pinched end of the core into the hollow fid end. Insert it into the coat at the T and work it through the coat as far as you can without a struggle. Depending on the size of the eye, the fid may not reach the necessary exit point in one pass. If this happens, bring the fid out of the coat, pulling some of the core with it. Then simply reinsert the fid into the *same* hole and work it farther through the coat. Continue this snaking process until the fid exits at Z. Be sure not to snag any strands of coat with the fid at reentry points.

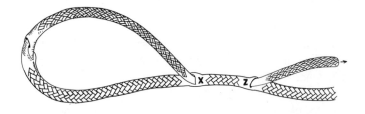

Draw up the slack until the coat-to-core unions formed at T and two hash marks meet at the top of the eye. Now that this portion of the splice is complete, you should hide the end of the coat by smoothing the coat from T to three hash marks. Take your time and be thorough so the tapered end slides completely into the core at the three hash marks.

Remove the fid and smooth the pucker. Poke through the coat at X to make some visible mark on the core inside. Also mark the core where it exits from Z. Pull on the core tail until the mark you made under X exits from the coat at Z. Unbraid the tail, comb, and fan it; then cut it off at a 45-degree angle between the two marks. Hold the rope gently at the union, and ease the coat from there around the eye until the core tail disappears. Trim ends.

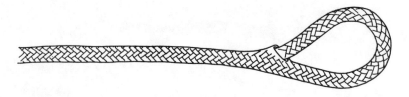

Take a firm grip of the rope close to the Slip Knot or attach it with a hook to a firm surface. If you measured carefully from the beginning of the splice, there should be enough slack in the bunched coat to roll down over the tail end and the coat-to-core joints.

Bunching may occur at the throat as the doubled core section and displaced yarns are distributed. If it does, roll and flex the rope or gently tug on the tail of the core. Begin this process gently but firmly. As you proceed, you may have to exert more pressure, perhaps to the point of pounding on the throat with a wooden mallet.

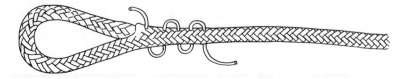

Double-braid splices—like most splices—are easy to take apart because they are designed to be pulled on, not pushed. To hold this splice firm, lock stitch it in the following way:

Pass a needle threaded with twine all the way through the throat, leaving a tail of about 8 inches. Make three complete stitches running along the standing part of the rope. Remove the needle from the twine and thread it with the tail end. Sew three stitches parallel to the first, but 90 degrees around the rope's circumference from them. Bring the two ends together through the standing part of the rope and tie with a Square Knot, shown in Chapter 13.

Turn the rope 90 degrees and repeat the stitches. Trim the twine ends.

End-to-End Splice

Here is a way to make an endless
loop or to join pieces of double-braid rope.

TOOLS AND MATERIALS

Double-braid rope
Tubular fid
Vinyl tape
Scissors or sharp knife
Marking pen
Needle

To make an endless loop in double-braid rope, you should allow four full fid lengths of rope to accommodate the splice. See page 9 for the relationship between rope diameter and fid size. Do not use double braid for an endless loop smaller than 2½ feet in circumference; for those splices, use 3-strand twisted, 8-plait, or 12-plait rope.

For maximum strength of an end-to-end splice, it is essential that the smooth, one-to-one relationship between coat and core be restored as completely as possible. This can be difficult, but pounding on the rope with a wooden mallet will loosen the strands and ease the job.

On each piece, draw the coat down over the working end of the core, removing as much slack as possible from the coat. Cut each end so that the coat and core are the same length, and tape to prevent unlaying.

Measure six full tubular fid lengths from each end and tie a Slip Knot.

Measure one full fid length from each end and label these reference points with an R. (Short and long fid lengths are marked on tubular fids; for the measurements in inches, see page 9.)

Mark an X one short fid length up the standing part of each rope from R.

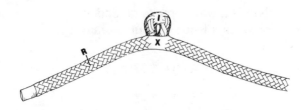

At X, gently push aside the strands of the coat to expose its inner core. Pull out a small loop of core through the coat as carefully as possible, and draw a single hash mark across the top of the core.

Pull out the working-end core completely at X and tape its end. Smooth the coat and core to confirm that the X and hash mark are aligned at equal distances from the end. Now pull out more core, this time from the standing part of the rope, and measure one short fid length from the single hash mark. Draw two hash marks there.

Continue along the core, pulling out more from the standing part if necessary, and mark three hash marks at a distance totaling one full fid length plus one short fid length from the two-hash mark point.

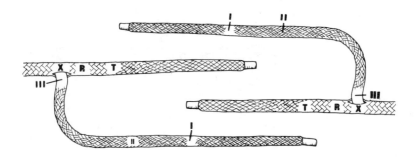

Repeat with the second rope.

To taper the coats, work with each separately. From R, toward the working end, count off seven sets of pics, or parallel ribs, that run clockwise and mark this spot with a T. Continue to work toward the end, placing a dot at *every other* clockwise pic until five have been marked so you will know where to cut.

Beginning again at T, mark every other counterclockwise pic.

Cut and remove the marked strands between T and the working end. Untape the end while pulling the strand loose. Repeat with the second rope.

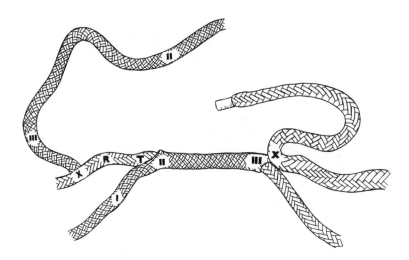

Pinch the taped end of either coat and insert it into the hollow end of the fid; tape it in place. Push the fid into the core of the *other* rope at two hash marks and out at three hash marks, being careful not to twist the coat. While holding the core, pull until the T is aligned with the two hash marks. Some bunching of the core will occur, but this will resolve itself later.

Repeat this procedure with the second rope.

Each core must now be reinserted into the coat that runs through its center. Tape the pinched end of either core into the hollow fid end

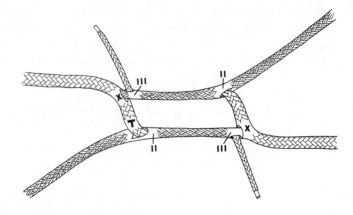

and insert the fid at T. Work it through the coat and exit at X. Repeat with the other rope.

Draw up the slack by pulling on both core and coat tails until the coat-to-core crossovers are snug.

Hold the rope at a joint and smooth all the puckered braid, working in both directions away from the joint. Take your time and be thorough so the tapered end of the coat slides completely into the core at three hash marks. Remove the fid from the core tail. Repeat with the second joint.

Cut off the core tails flush at the coat.

Take a firm grip of the rope close to a slip knot. If you measured carefully from the beginning of the splice, there should be enough slack in the coat to pull down over one of the coat-to-core joints and the tail ends. Repeat to cover the second joint with slack from the opposite direction.

Bunching may occur as all the extra yarns running through the coat are distributed. If it does, roll and flex the rope. Begin this process gently but firmly, gradually applying more pressure as necessary. You may have to pound the rope with a wooden mallet.

An opening through the splice is normal, but it should not be any longer than the diameter of the rope.

End Splice

A neat alternative to whipping a double-braid rope end.

TOOLS AND MATERIALS

Double-braid rope
Tubular fid
Vinyl tape or whipping twine
Scissors or sharp knife
Marking pen

If the end of the rope has been heat-sealed, cut it off and tape it to keep it from unlaying. Measure one full fid length from the working end of the rope and mark this spot with an X.

Move up the rope at least five full fid lengths and tie a tight Slip Knot.

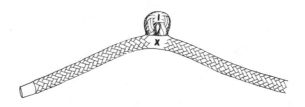

Return to the X and gently push aside the strands of the coat to expose its inner core. Pull out a small loop of core through the coat as carefully as possible, and make a single hash mark across the top of the core. Pull out the core completely and tape its end. Confirm that the X and hash mark are aligned at equal distances from the end.

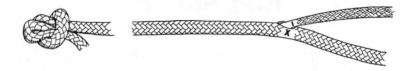

Now pull out more core, this time from the standing part of the rope, and measure one short fid length from the single hash mark. (Short and long fid lengths are marked on tubular fids; for the measurement in inches, see page 9.) Make two hash marks there.

Continue along the core, pulling out more from the standing part of the rope if necessary, and make three hash marks at a distance totaling one full fid length plus one short fid length from the two hash marks.

Now draw the rope's outer coat into its core. Remember that the coat is marked with letters, the core with hash marks. Pinch the taped

end of the coat and insert it into the hollow end of the fid; tape it in place. Push the fid into the core at two hash marks and out at three. Be careful not to twist the coat. Pull until the splice is snug but not buckled.

Remove the fid and tape. To taper the coat tail, unbraid and fan it, then mark one-third of a full fid length up the coat. Cut at an angle from the opposite bottom corner.

Smooth the core, working from two hash marks to three hash marks; if you measured carefully, the coat tail will slip into the core.

Starting from the Slip Knot work the coat down over the core, pulling an ever-deepening fold into the coat ahead of your fingers. When you reach the end, the fold you have created should be deep enough to envelope the entire splice, and the crease of the fold where it terminates at the working end of the splice will appear like the half-inverted finger of a rubber glove when you slip it off your hand.

Cut the core off flush with the coat. Smooth again to ensure that any exposed core is completely covered.

Rope-to-Wire Splice

A Rope-to-Wire Splice is often
used to attach rigging wire to a halyard.
With double-braid rope, both the core
and coat must be spliced into the wire.

TOOLS AND MATERIALS

Double-braid rope
7x19 Stainless steel wire
Swedish fid
Wire cutters
Vinyl tape
Scissors or sharp knife
Hot knife or flame source
Ruler
Waxed whipping twine
Marking pen

The 7x19 stainless steel wire comprises six strands, each containing 19 yarns, and a central core. The wire should be suitable for rigging and should measure about one-half the rope's diameter.

For this splice, the wire must be tapered to a core plus one strand.

Cut one strand at 6 inches from the end, cut one at 5 inches, one at 4 inches and two at 3 inches. Tape around the wire at each level.

Tie a Slip Knot 8 feet up the braided rope to keep the coat from creeping up the core more than necessary. If the end of the rope has been heat-sealed, cut it off; push the coat 4 feet up the core. Cut off 6 inches of the exposed core and tape the end.

Measure up the core 21 inches and mark.

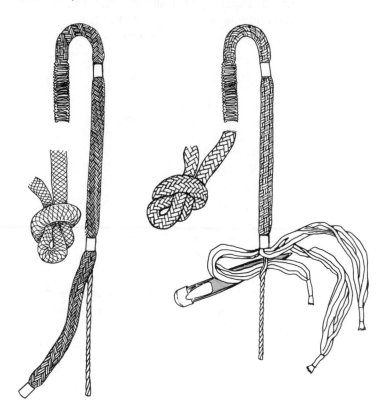

Insert the tip of the tapered wire into the hollow core 8 inches from the working end and gently and carefully work it up through the core until it reaches the mark at 21 inches.

Tape lightly around the core and wire at the 21-inch and 8-inch locations to hold your work snug.

Working carefully, unbraid the core to the 8-inch mark and divide the yarns into three groups. You will get a much neater splice if you tape neighboring yarns together.

To splice the first group of yarns into the wire, slip the fid under two wire strands in the direction *opposite* the twist of the wire. Lay the rope along the groove from the handle to the tip; pull the rope into place and remove the tool. Repeat with the other two yarn groups, carrying on around the back of the wire to make a complete wrap with each group. Continue until three rounds of tucks are completed. Remove one-third of each group and tuck the fourth round; remove another third and tuck the fifth round. Cut the ends very close.

Melt any ends into the wire by passing a lighted match *close* to the cut ends. Use some caution here, or you could melt your whole splice.

Beginning at the Slip Knot, milk the coat by squeezing it while sliding your hand gradually toward the wire. Work in short, overlapping sections, and do not pull on the coat. When you have removed all slack, the core-to-wire portion of the splice should be completely covered. Whip over the coat where the splice on the core ends. (Instructions for whipping are given in Chapter 11.)

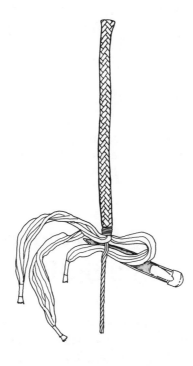

For the coat-to-wire portion of the splice, unbraid the coat, smooth the yarns out straight, and as you did previously with the core, divide the yarns into three groups. These groups must also be spliced into the wire, but they will be inserted so they travel in the *same* direction as the wire strands. Insert each group under the appropriate wire strand pair, completing one round of tucks.

To taper this splice, repeat the tucks, omitting a portion of each yarn group at each tuck, until only a few yarns remain. Cut the ends close to the wire and carefully melt the yarn ends with a match.

Core-to-Core Eye Splice

Use this alternative Eye Splice
on double-braid rope such as Kevlar, for
which, according to manufacturer
specifications, the primary strength
lies in the core.

TOOLS AND MATERIALS

Double-braid rope
Tubular fid
Vinyl tape
Scissors or sharp knife
Marking pen
Waxed whipping twine
Needle
Thimble (optional)

Place a fresh piece of tape on the rope end where the eye is to be spliced to keep the rope from unlaying. Using a tubular fid, measure two full fid lengths from the tape and label this reference point with an R.

Add the amount of rope necessary to form the eye, or for the loop around the thimble, if one is used. Mark an X here, at the throat of the splice. (This is a complicated splice to complete with a thimble, so measurements are critical.)

Move up the rope at least eight full fid lengths and tie a tight Slip Knot.

Return to the X and gently push aside the strands of the coat to expose its inner core. Pull out a small loop of core through the coat as carefully as possible. Draw a single hash mark across the top of the core.

Pull out the working-end core completely, and tape its end.

Now pull out more core, this time from the standing part of the rope, and measure one short fid length from the single hash mark. Make two hash marks there.

Continue along the core three full fid lengths plus one short fid length, pulling out more core if necessary. Make three hash marks.

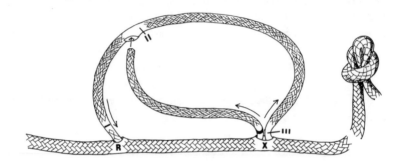

The distance between I and II is one short fid length

The distance between II and III is three full
fid lengths plus one short fid length

Pinch the taped end of the core and insert it into the hollow end of the fid; tape it in place. Push the fid into the coat at R and out at X. You should now have the core exiting twice at X. Pull the core through until the single hash mark lines up with R, then hold it firmly in position while you smooth the coat from R to X. Mark the tail core where it exits at X with a band around the core.

Insert the fid (with the core end still taped to it) into the core at the two hash marks, run it through the core, and pull it out at the three hash marks, in effect pulling the core through itself. Pull until the band lines up with the two hash marks.

To taper the tail that exits at the three hash marks, fan it, then measure from its working end one-third of a full fid length, making a mark at that point. Cut at an angle from the opposite bottom corner to the place marked.

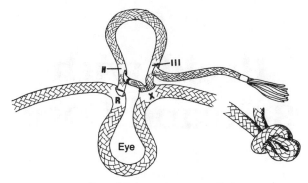

Core disappears into coat at X

Hold the rope where the band on the core and the two hash marks meet and smooth the core toward the loose tail. The tail should slip into the core if your measurements were correct.

Attach the Slip Knot to a sturdy hook, or have an assistant hold it. Smooth the coat from the knot toward the splice until the whole core is enveloped by the coat, taking special care around the eye.

Detach the Slip Knot from the hook, and attach the eye there instead.

Pull both the standing part of the rope and the coat tail (from R to the working end) toward you tightly.

Apply a tight layer of tape around the throat for a distance equal to one short fid length.

Apply a tight whipping over the tape (see Chapter 11).

Cut the tail close.

5

Braid with 3-Strand Core

Braided rope with 3-strand core can also be called 16-plait with 3-strand core, because the outer coat comprises 16 braids. I like Marlowbraid's fuzzy coat; it provides a good grip and at the same time feels good in my hands. Technically a two-part rope, it is unlike double braid because 90 percent of its strength is in its twisted core.

This is a difficult rope to splice, but the results are worth the extra effort. Don't attempt to splice any rope of this type under ¼ inch in diameter, because the Marlow splicing tool (see page 9) won't fit; for smaller rope, use the Sew and Serve Splice in Chapter 12.

Eye Splice

TOOLS AND MATERIALS

Braid with 3-strand core
Marlow splicing tool
Scissors or sharp knife
Vinyl tape
Marking pen
Ruler
Whipping twine
Thimble (optional)
Swedish fid

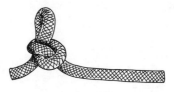

Tie a Slip Knot about 5 feet from the end of the rope to prevent the coat from creeping up the core more than necessary. If the end of the rope has been heat-sealed, cut it off and tape the new end to prevent unlaying.

Mark the coat 9 inches from the end to make room in the working end for the splice. Form the rope into an eye and mark the coat again. (Allow an extra half inch if you are using a thimble.)

Push aside the threads of the coat at your second mark until the hole is large enough to expose the core. Extract the core by hooking it with a Swedish fid. Cut 3 inches off the core's end.

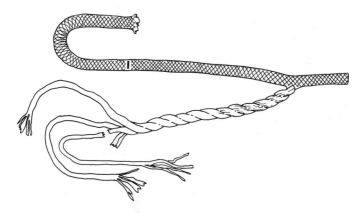

Form the eye to the proper size, this time on the core, and cut off one of the core's three twisted strands at the throat of the splice.

Move toward the working end an inch or so, and remove *half* the thickness of another strand. Tape. Continue tapering and taping until

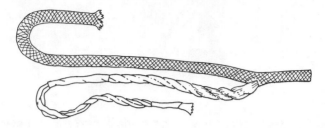

the end of the core is small enough to go through the eye of the splic-ing tool.

To ease the coat away from the core and make the splice easier to complete, draw out additional core from the standing part of the rope. Extract about 3 inches for 5/16- and 3/8-inch rope, and 4 inches for 7/16- and 1/2-inch rope.

Begin at the Slip Knot to reposition the coat by milking it firmly while sliding your hand toward the spot where the coat and core separate. This action loosens the core and coat and makes them easier to work with. Work in short, overlapping sections and do not pull on the coat.

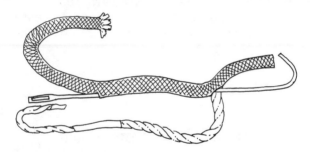

Insert the eye of the Marlow splicing tool (see page 9) into the coat where it opens for the core. Push it through the coat to exit at the throat.

Thread the core through the eye of the splicing tool and draw it back through the coat to exit with the tool at the coat opening.

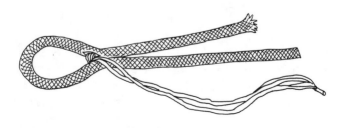

You will now gradually work all of the core ends farther down the standing part of the rope. Untape the ends, unlay the tail, comb out the strands with your fingers, and divide the yarns into three groups. Tape the ends of the new groupings.

Insert the eye of the splicing tool 12 inches below the mark for the throat and exit at the original coat opening. Thread one third of the tail, located there, into the eye. Pull it through the coat and draw it out.

Repeat with the remaining two sections of core tail, bringing one out 10 inches below the throat and the other out 8 inches below the throat, pulling each time. Remove the tape from all three sections.

Pull until the union is firm and the throat closes.

Taper the coat tail by removing one strand at 3 inches from the end, two strands at 2 inches, and four strands at 1 inch.

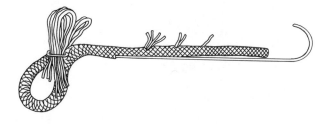

Now the working end of the coat must be pulled through the standing part of the rope. To make it easier to do this, begin a pathway by inserting the empty tool at the throat and pushing it out about 3 inches up the standing part of the rope. Wiggle it.

Reverse the tool, entering the rope 3 inches below the throat and exiting at the throat. Lace the eye with some of the shortest pieces of coat tail and pull them through. Repeat at various points around the circumference, 3 inches below the throat. Pull the longer tail pieces through farther from the throat.

If you are using a thimble, insert it now. To take the slack out of the splice, hook the eye over a strong hook or knob, hold the core and cover tails, and pull firmly until the coat and core are snug.

Cut off the tails close to their exit points and firmly smooth the entire coat over the core from the slip knot to the throat. The clipped ends should slip into the rope.

Rope-to-Wire Splice

This is a good splice to attach rigging wire to a halyard.

TOOLS AND MATERIAL

Braid with 3-strand core
7x19 Stainless steel wire
Swedish fid
Wire cutters
Vinyl tape
Scissors or sharp knife
Hot knife or flame source
Waxed whipping twine
Marking pen
Ruler

The 7x19 stainless steel wire comprises six strands, each containing 19 yarns, and a central core. The wire should be suitable for rigging and should measure about one-half the rope's diameter.

For this splice, the wire must be tapered to a core plus one strand. Cut one strand at 6 inches from the end, one at 5 inches, one at 4 inches, and two at 3 inches. Tape around the wire at each level.

Tie a slip knot 8 feet up the braided rope to keep the coat from creeping up the core more than necessary. If the end of the rope has been heat-sealed, cut it off; push the coat 4 feet up the core, cut off 6 inches of the exposed core, and tape the end.

Measure 21 inches up the core, and tape.

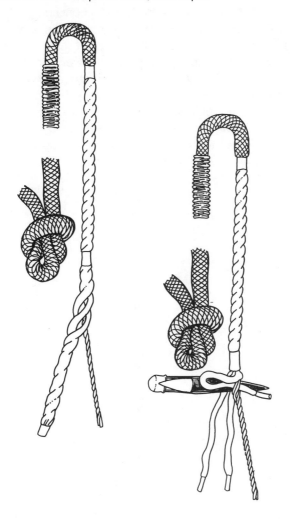

At that point, open the lay and set the tip of tapered wire into the rope's twisted core at a 45-degree angle. Spiral the wire into the lay of the core, continuing to within 6 inches of the working end. Tape into position. Unlay the core strands from here to the working end.

To splice the first rope strand into the wire, slip the fid under two wire strands in the direction *opposite* the twist of the wire. Lay the rope strand along the groove from the handle to the tip; pull the rope into place and remove the tool. For a more finished appearance, untwist the core strand as it passes under the wires.

Repeat with the other two core strands, continuing in a direction opposite the lay of the wires. Each core strand tucks under a different pair of wire strands, just as in a 3-strand rope splice. Continue until five rounds of tucks are completed; cut the ends very close.

Beginning at the slip knot, milk the coat by squeezing it while sliding your hand gradually toward the wire. Work in short, overlapping sections, and do not pull on the coat. When you have removed all slack, the core-to-wire portion of the splice should be completely covered. Whip over the coat where the splice on the core ends. (Instructions for whipping are given in Chapter 11.)

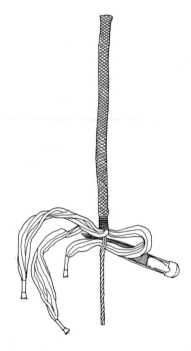

For the coat-to-wire portion of this splice, untwist the coat back to the whipping and divide the yarns into three groups, trying to keep neighboring yarns together. These yarns must also be spliced into the wire, but they will be inserted so they twist in the *same* direction as the wire.

To taper the end, repeat the tucks, omitting one yarn at each tuck until only 7 or 8 yarns remain in each group.

Cut the ends close to the wire.

6

Braid with Parallel Core

Parallel fibers wrapped in a gauze-like material form the core of this braid. When low stretch and high strength are critical, such as in a halyard, this rope is a good choice; if flexibility is important, double braid is better.

Eye Splice

The basic directions for this splice provide
a soft eye that conforms easily to small blocks.
A variation, as noted in the text below,
produces a hard, unyielding eye that is excellent
for situations calling for a larger loop.
These directions are for Sta-Set X, manufactured
by New England Ropes, Inc., of New Bedford,
Massachusetts, the major distributor of this rope
to the marine market; other braid with
parallel core requires a different splice.
A special splicing tool, the Uni-fid (see page 9),
is necessary to complete this splice because
of the rope's parallel-strand core. Chandleries
that stock this rope usually sell the fid also.

TOOLS AND MATERIALS

Braid with parallel core
Uni-fid
Scissors or sharp knife
Masking tape
Waxed whipping twine
Marking pen

Place a fresh piece of tape on the rope end where the eye is to be spliced to keep the rope from unlaying.

Tie a slip knot 12 full fid lengths from the working end to retain the one-to-one relationship between core and coat.

Wrap a layer of tape around the rope one full fid length from the working end. (Fid sections are marked on the shipping tube for the tool.) Label this reference point R.

Add the amount of rope necessary to form the eye, and mark this spot X.

Continuing toward the slip knot, measure 1½ full fid lengths. (Note that one-half of a full fid length is *not* the same as a short fid length.) Mark this point Y.

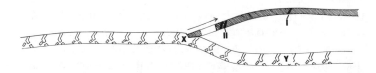

Return to the X and gently push aside the strands of the coat to expose its inner core. Pull out a small loop using the Uni-fid. Draw a single hash mark across the top of the core.

Pull out the working-end core completely, taper the end by cutting it at an angle, and tape. This will ease snaking of the core through the coat in a succeeding step.

Now pull out more core, this time from the standing part of the rope, and measure one short fid length from the hash mark. Place two hash marks there.

For a *soft* eye: Place a layer of tape on the standing side of this spot so it just touches the double hash mark.

For a *hard* eye: Measure from the two hash marks toward the working end of the core, the distance between R and X (rope set aside for the eye). Place a layer of tape on the standing side of this spot.

Sink the hook of the Uni-fid into the wrapped core 1½ inches from the tapered end. To prevent snagging, apply a smooth layer of tape to hold the fid in place on the core.

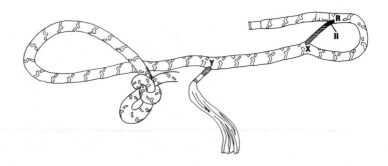

Insert the free end of the fid into the coat at R and work it past X, then out through the coat at Y. Use two hands, massaging the rope ahead of the fid. If you snag the core, back up to free it, and then proceed.

Remove the fid.

Unwind the gauze wrapping from around the parallel fibers of the tail between the tape placed for the eye and the working end and cut if off, taking care not to cut any of the core fibers. Measure one short fid length from the working end and mark. Fan the tail and make an angled cut from the mark to the end to give a full taper to the core.

To taper the coat tail, begin at R and count down five pics, or ridges, and mark. Continuing toward the working end, count off 15 pics and mark again. Cut the tail off square there. Unlay the coat back to the mark at the fifth pic, and make an angled cut from the fifth to the fifteenth pic.

Align R and two hash marks, causing the core strands to begin creeping into the coat. (Bunching usually prevents the strands from disappearing, but if they totally slip into the coat at this step, that's okay.)

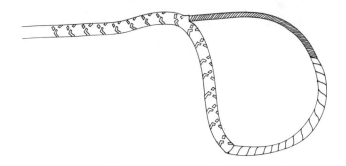

Tightly tape the tapered coat tail to the core with masking tape; use as little tape as possible, but be sure to get all the loose ends. Smooth the coat from the slip knot down toward the eye; the core should slide back into the coat.

Attach the slip knot to a mounted hook, or have a friend hold it. Smooth the coat over the core and coat-to-core joint. Begin gently, but if bunching occurs at the throat, roll and flex the area. If the coat does not move into position, use more muscle power and less finesse. You may have to pound on the rope with a wooden mallet to redistribute the strands.

Lock stitch the splice into place. (See Chapter 4, Eye Splice, for directions.)

7

Hollow Braid

Splices in hollow braid work on the same principle as the Chinese finger puzzle. After the working end is passed through the braid of the standing part and into the hollow of the rope, and the fid is removed, the strands of the braid return to their factory form. In doing so, they constrict, gripping the length of rope tightly.

A special splicing tool, or fid, is made for this rope, but these fids are hard to find, so I recommend an alternative—a knitting needle with its endcap removed, or even a length of wire coat hanger. Either can be taped tightly to the rope while you work.

Eye Splice

TOOLS AND MATERIALS

Hollow-braid rope
Splicing tool (see chapter introduction)
Scissors or sharp knife
Marking pen

No exact measurements are needed to splice this rope, but for an eye or loop 3 inches or smaller, use the Locked Eye Splice later in this chapter.

Lay out your rope and form the necessary loop. For splicing ropes of ¼ to ½ inch (the most commonly used sizes) allow about 1½ to 2 feet for the tail.

Taper the end of the rope by cutting it at a 45-degree angle. Pinch this tapered end into the hollow of the fid or slide it like a sleeve over the knitting needle or piece of coat hanger and tape it tightly.

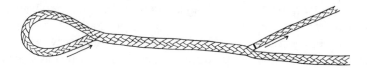

Insert the splicing tool through the braid at the throat of the splice. Ease the tip of the tool down through the hollow of the rope for a distance of 8 or 9 inches, then poke it back out through the braid and draw the tool completely out, pulling the tail through to adjust the eye to the desired size. Smooth the rope.

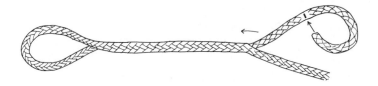

Pick up the tailpiece with the splicing tool attached and mark it where it exits the braid. Then pull on the tail until an additional 3 inches is showing, in effect shrinking the eye. Doubling the tailpiece back on itself, insert the tool at the mark on the tail and run it back down the tail hollow 2½ to 3 inches before pushing it back out through the braid.

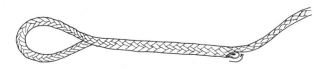

Pull the end through until the loop you have just formed in the tail disappears.

Cut the end close to the braid and push the cut strand ends back into the tail and out of sight.

Smooth the coat back into place.

Finally, work the tail back into the standing part so that the eye grows back to its proper size, noting as you go the unique property that causes this splice to hold: If you grasp the eye in one hand and hold the standing part of the rope in the other, the weave of the braid around the spliced section will tighten when you try to pull the tail back into the core, and the tail will refuse to budge. If you grasp the eye in one hand while pinching the braid opening in the throat of the splice with your other thumb and forefinger, you can easily pull the tail back through the braid until just its knobby end remains visible. Anyone who has ever played with a Chinese finger puzzle will understand why this works as it does.

Locked Eye Splice

**This is an easy and quick splice
to execute. It is a good method to use
if the eye is 3 inches or smaller.**

TOOLS AND MATERIALS

Hollow-braid rope
Splicing tool (see chapter introduction)
Scissors or sharp knife

Lay out your rope and form the necessary eye. For rope of ¼ to ½ inch in diameter, allow about 10 inches for the tail.
Taper the end of the rope by cutting the tip off at a 45-degree angle.

Push the tapered end into the hollow of the fid or affix it tightly to the splicing tool as described for the previous splice.
Wrap the working end of the rope around the standing part to make

a half hitch as shown in the drawing, and adjust the hitch until the eye is the desired size.

Insert the tip of the splicing tool into the standing part of the rope just above the hitch and ease the tool approximately 8 inches up through the standing part's core before poking back out through the braid. Pull the tool completely out and draw out the tail until snug.

Smooth the rope and cut the tail off close, tucking the cut strand ends back into the braid of the standing part until hidden from view.

End-to-End Splice

**Use this splice to join two ends of
hollow-braid rope or to form an endless loop.**

TOOLS AND MATERIALS

Hollow-braid rope
Splicing tool (see chapter introduction)
Scissors or sharp knife

Lay out the two ends of rope, or, if you are making an endless loop, adjust it to the correct size. For rope of ¼ to ½ inch in diameter, allow about 10 inches for each tail.

Taper both ends by cutting the tips off at a 45-degree angle.

Push one tapered end into the hollow of the fid or affix it tightly to the splicing tool, as described for the Eye Splice in this chapter.

Measure 10 inches from the other working end and insert the splicing tool at this point, easing it up the hollow core of the standing part for 10 inches.

Bring the tool back out through the braid, trim the end close, and tuck the strand ends back into the braid and out of sight.

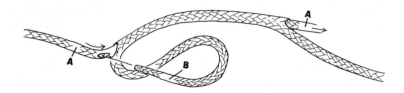

Repeat for the other tail, inserting the splicing tool as shown in the drawing.

This splice will hold in use and is similar to the Chinese finger puzzle principle described for the Eye Splice in this chapter.

8-Plait Rope

This rope is laid with eight strands that are worked in pairs for splice strength and appearance. If the manufacturer has not differentiated the two right-laid pairs from the two left-laid pairs, mark either pair with a pen to simplify the splicing process. (Directions are given with each splice for the length of rope to mark.)

Eye Splice

TOOLS AND MATERIALS

8-Plait rope
Swedish fid
Vinyl tape
Scissors or sharp knife
Hot knife or heat source
Marking pen
Waxed whipping twine

Estimate the amount of rope you will need for the eye and mark either both right-laid strand pairs or both left-laid strand pairs for about twice this distance. Starting from the working end, count up the stand-

ing part of the rope 10 pics and seize the rope at that point with tape or twine.

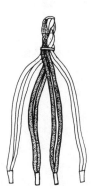

Unlay the rope to the seizing, allowing the twist in the individual strands to remain, and tape the strand pairs together at their working ends.

Form the eye and take a painted pair of strands and tuck them

at the throat under a handy unpainted pair in the standing part. A Swedish fid can make the process easier.

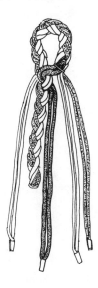

Turn the splice over and slip the other painted pair under the second unpainted pair. Always work so that you are tucking against the lay of the strands in the standing part. That is, if the standing pair twists from upper right to lower left, tuck under it from left to right.

Turn your work a third time, and tuck an unpainted strand pair under a painted pair; turn, then tuck the second unpainted pair under the second painted pair. One round of tucks is now finished.

Complete *at least* two more rounds of tucks.

Cut off one strand from each pair 1 or 2 inches from the end. Tape or heat seal the ends. Tuck the remaining single strands twice more, then cut and tape.

End-to-End Splice

TOOLS AND MATERIALS

8-Plait rope (2 pieces)
Swedish fid
Vinyl tape
Marking pen
Waxed whipping twine

Seize each rope tightly at the ninth or tenth pic. Mark both right-laid strand pairs or both left-laid strand pairs from the bitter end of each rope to about the sixteenth pic, remove the tape or heat-sealed tips at the working ends, and unlay the strand pairs, leaving the twist in each strand. Tape the strand pairs at their ends, taking care that they do not become twisted together.

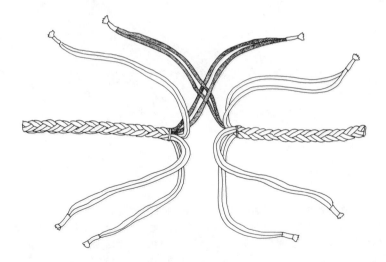

Align the ropes end-to-end. To marry the ropes, lace a painted pair of strands from the right-hand rope through the corresponding painted pair on the other rope as shown in the illustration.

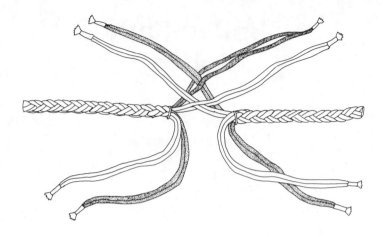

Lace the adjacent unpainted pair on the right-hand rope through the corresponding pair on the other rope.

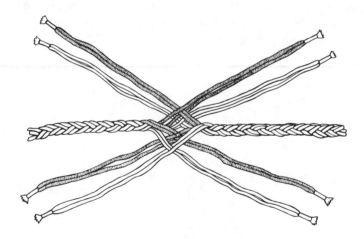

The other two strand pairs are laced in the opposite way: The painted pair on the left-hand rope is laced through the corresponding painted pair on the right-hand rope, and finally the left-hand unpainted pair is laced through the last, opposite strand pair.

Draw the two rope ends together and tie with twine at the center to hold the developing splice in place. Remove the original seizings.

To begin the first round of tucks, insert one painted pair under the adjacent unpainted pair on the standing part of the mated rope and

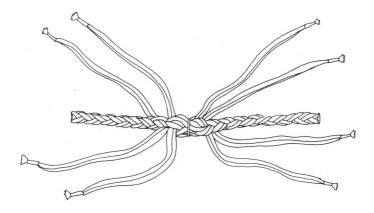

cinch tightly, then insert a pair of unpainted strands under the neighboring painted pair. Continue in this manner until 1½ inches of strands remain, and then repeat the procedure for the other side.

Cut off one strand from each pair. Tape or heat seal the ends. Tuck the remaining single strands twice more, then cut and tape.

Temporary Eye Splice

This is a temporary Eye Splice that is dependable and quick to execute. To be on the safe side, replace it with a standard Eye Splice at an early opportunity.

TOOLS AND MATERIALS

8-Plait rope
Swedish fid
Vinyl tape
Scissors or sharp knife

Measure off 12 inches for the splice, and beginning there, form the eye. At the throat, with the point of the fid, separate the strands into clockwise and counterclockwise groups.

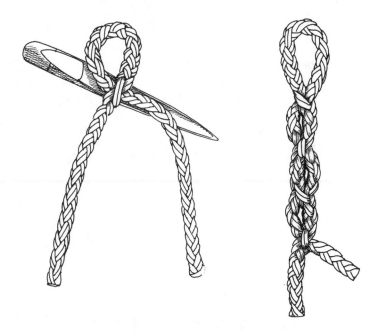

Reeve, or insert, the tail end through the opening by the fid. Move down three pics along the standing part from where the tail emerges, separate the strands in the same way as before, and reeve the tail back through in the opposite direction. Repeat this process twice.

Tape the tail to the standing part. The tail should be at least 3 inches to allow for slippage.

9

8-Plait Rope-to-Chain Splice

Technically, this splice belongs in the chapter on 8-plait rope, but it deserves a chapter of its own. This splice is superior to other systems for anchor rodes, because there is no knobby shackle and thimble connection to drag across the deck. Also, it eliminates a shackle in a position where the pin often is lost from chafe or rust.

Chain is used on an anchor rode more for its weight than its strength. It lies on the bottom and helps to convert the force pulling on the anchor from vertical to horizontal so the anchor will be less likely to break out of the bottom, and more likely to hold. Chain is also more resistant to chafing on rocks and coral heads. Match your chain to the anchor and shackle, as recommended by your supplier, and choose rope of sufficient diameter to be handled comfortably and to match the breaking strength of the chain. Be careful, however, not to buy rope so big that the strand pairs can't be laced through the chain links. Make sure the rope is nylon, which is elastic enough to function as a shock absorber when the boat bucks and tugs at its anchor.

Rope-to-Chain Splice

The Rope-to-Chain splice and the construction
of the 8-plait rope work very well together
for anchor rodes, permitting the passage of rope
and chain through a bow chock or hawsepipe.
The 8-plait rope is excellent: kinks and hockles
fall right out, so it need not be coiled
belowdecks. If 8-plait rope is not available,
12-plait can be used instead; no shackle is needed.
Be sure to work this splice up tight; excess
slack in the spliced strands could cause abrasion.

TOOLS AND MATERIALS

8-Plait rope
Chain
Sharp knife or scissors
Electrical friction tape
Serving mallet or reel-type serving tool
Whipping twine
Liquid rope seal (optional)

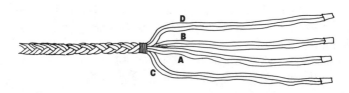

Measure the length of 12 links of chain to determine the required
splice length for the rope. As an example, this distance is about 12
inches for 3/16-inch chain. Pick up the 8-plait rope and measure the
appropriate distance from the working end. Apply a good tight whipping (see Chapter 11) at that point and unlay the rope back to the whipping. Notice the construction of the rope—four pairs of strands, each

pair comprising one strand of yarns twisted clockwise and one with yarns twisted counterclockwise.

Lay out the rope as shown.

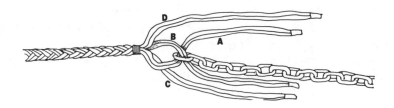

Set the first link of chain directly on top of strand pair A, and lace these two strands up through the link. Lace strand pair B down through the link, making sure it crosses pair A.

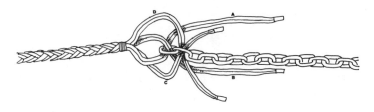

Repeat this procedure with strand pairs C and D through the second link, then return to pairs A and B for the third link, and so on. In this fashion, leapfrog down the chain. Two strand pairs cross through

each link, and each pair skips a link before entering another from the side on which it exited in the previous pass.

Continue this two-part process until 10 links have been filled, then

finish the splice on the eleventh and twelfth links. To finish, remove the tape from the strand-pair ends. Separate the two strands of each pair, pass one through a link (either the eleventh or the twelfth, as appropriate) and the other around the side of the same link, then seize the two strands together closely, as shown, to prevent movement of the rope over the chain. Seal the strands by melting with a match or hot knife. Applying a coat of liquid rope sealer would be a plus. As a final touch, serve the entire splice tightly with small stuff (see Chapter 12) to further ensure that the strands do not chafe.

10

12-Plait Rope

This rope is used primarily on commercial boats for hawsers, docklines, and tow lines. There is no need to coil 12-plait; you can drop it in a heap and then just give it one or two good shakes to rid it of hockles and kinks.

Eye Splice

This splice can be completed with your fingers, but a fid will do a neater job.

TOOLS AND MATERIALS

12-Plait rope
Swedish fid
Vinyl tape
Scissors or sharp knife

The amount of rope necessary for this splice equals the circumference of the rope times 7. Determine this distance from the working end and tape the rope there. Unlay enough rope to be able to tape each of the 12 strand ends, and then unlay the rope to the tape, taking care to retain the individual twists.

Form the eye above the tape and mark the throat.

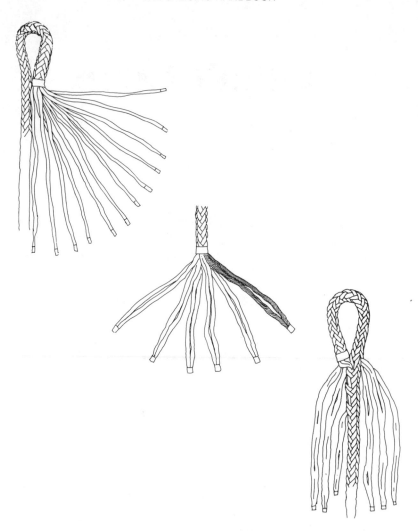

Group the strands into six pairs, each pair having one strand with its yarns twisting up and to the right and an adjacent strand twisting up and to the left. Tape the pairs together.

Divide the six strands into two groups, taking the three strand pairs on one side (to the left in the drawing) and reeving them directly through the middle of the rope at the mark on the throat. It is important to maintain the twist on the strands as they pass through the rope, and they must lay just right—not too loose or too tight. Snug the strands to remove excess slack.

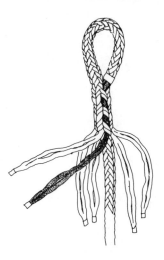

Begin with a convenient strand pair and tuck it under a nearby strand pair in the standing part of the rope and then over one strand.

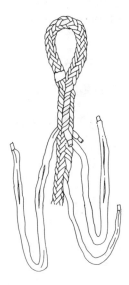

Repeat with the five remaining pairs, making each tuck parallel with the one adjacent.

Complete two more rounds of tucks, then begin tapering by trimming every other strand pair about 1½ inches from the standing part of the rope.

Complete another three rounds of tucks with the remaining strand

pairs, then taper again, this time by cutting one strand from each pair. Retape the ends.

After another three rounds of tucks, draw up the three single strands tightly. Cut and tape their ends, leaving tails of about 1½ inches.

End-to-End Splice

TOOLS AND MATERIALS

12-Plait rope
Swedish fid
Vinyl tape
Scissors or sharp knife

As in the 12-Plait Eye Splice, the amount of rope necessary for this splice equals the circumference of the rope times 7 (for each rope). Determine this figure, and tape both ropes at that distance from the working ends. Unlay enough rope to be able to tape the 12 strand ends on each rope to prevent the yarns from raveling, and unlay the ropes to the tape, taking care to retain the individual twist.

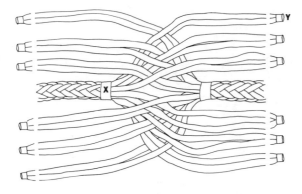

Distance from X and Y equals 7 times the rope circumference

Group the strands into six pairs for each rope, each pair having one strand with yarns that twist clockwise and an adjacent strand with yarns that twist counterclockwise. Tape the ends of each pair of strands together.

To join, or marry, the two ropes, begin with any strand pair on one rope and lace it through the corresponding pair on the second. Lace the neighboring pair on the second rope through the corresponding pair on the first. Proceed in this way until all the strands are laced. Gently snug the two pieces together by drawing up the strands.

To make the first round of tucks, pass any convenient strand pair over one nearby strand in the standing part of the other rope and draw it under the next two strands. Make parallel tucks with each subsequent strand pair to complete the first round.

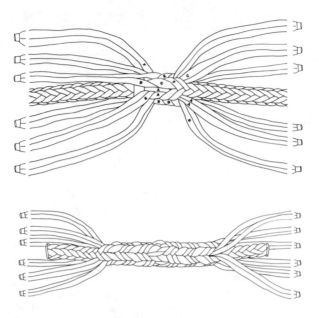

Repeat with the second rope. Then complete two more rounds of tucks, working in the same way.

To begin tapering, trim off every other strand pair about 1½ inches from the standing part of the rope and tape the ends.

Complete another three rounds of tucks and taper again, this time by cutting one strand from each pair. Retape the ends.

Complete three more rounds of tucks with the three single strands, then draw up the strands as you would a loose shoelace, until the pieces of rope lay together but are not overly tight or loose.

Tape the ends, leaving a tail of about 1½ inches.

11

Whipping and Seizing

Both whipping and seizing are methods for binding rope, but whipping prevents the end of a rope from unlaying, while seizing binds two pieces of rope together, side by side. A traditional whipping is a tight winding of waxed or tarred small stuff, the more modern alternative being an application of one or two coats of a specially formulated liquid adhesive. Most marine supply stores carry these materials, often in kit form.

For seizing, many people now use plastic ties, which provide a quick, inexpensive way to bundle rope. Traditional seizing, however, looks good and will not damage or mark the rope.

Traditional Whipping

The width of the whipping should approximate the diameter of the rope. It is best to have two whippings a short distance apart—one near the rope end and one a few rope diameters farther up the standing part—with the small stuff pulled tight on each. If one is loosened, the other should keep the end from unlaying.

TOOLS AND MATERIALS

Rope to be whipped
Small stuff: waxed whipping twine
Scissors or sharp knife
Vinyl tape
Hot knife or heat source

Tape the end of the rope or, if it is synthetic, heat-seal the end with a hot knife or other heat source until the yarns are fused.

Begin whipping at least an inch from the bitter end of the rope. Lay a loop of small stuff across the rope, leaving a tail of 5 or 6 inches on the bitter end. You will need to grasp this tail later, so don't cover the tail completely with whipping.

With the working piece of small stuff, wrap around the rope from the tail end toward the apex of the loop, covering the loop until the width of the whipping is at least as wide as the diameter of the rope.

To end the whipping, insert the working end of the small stuff through the loop. Pull on the bitter end, or tail, of the small stuff until the loop slides completely out of sight. Clip the ends close.

Sailmaker's Whipping

TOOLS AND MATERIALS

Rope to be whipped
Small stuff: waxed whipping twine
Sailmaker's needle

Take two stitches through the rope with the small stuff to secure its end, then wrap the small stuff around the rope, working back over the stitches, until the width of the whipping approximates the diameter of the rope.

Draw the working end of the small stuff under the entire length of the whipping, and pull it through.

Now bring the small stuff over the whipping (left to right in the illustration) to make the first angled stitch. Stitch through about one-third of the rope's girth, staying on the same side of the whipping.

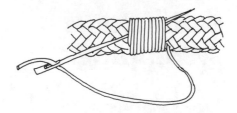

Rotate the rope 120 degrees. Bring the small stuff back across the whipping to make another angled stitch, parallel with the first but one-third of the rope's circumference removed. Stitch through the rope

again, and make a third angled stitch. Continue in this fashion until all the stitches are doubled, then clip the end.

Note: For 3-strand rope, the angled stitches follow the lay.

Seizing

TOOLS AND MATERIALS

Rope to be seized
Nylon small stuff

The size and construction of the small stuff are your choice.

Form a loop at the end of the small stuff and tuck the end two or three times through the lay of its standing part. if the ropes being seized are 3-strand, work in the direction opposite the lay.

Circle the ropes to be seized, and anchor the working end of the small stuff by threading it through the loop and doubling it back upon

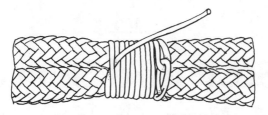

itself. Apply eight to ten tight wraps around the ropes, taking care to cover the tail.

Take a hitch, as shown, and working back across the seizing, place a layer of wraps over the first layer. These wraps are called riding turns, because they "ride" on the first layer. The riding turns should not be as tight as the original turns and should number one fewer.

Pass the working end through the original loop and wrap two turns across the seizing, between the two ropes; take up any slack.

Tie a Flat Knot (see illustration). Draw the knot tight and clip close.

12

Sew and Serve Eye Splice

Served ropework lends an air of tradition, and for the owner of a traditional vessel, a few of these splices aboard would add a nice touch of the old days.

This splice works very well for double-braid, 8-plait, and 12-plait rope. The splice requires a layer of serving; it is important that the sewing be very tight and the taper, very smooth.

TOOLS AND MATERIALS

Double-braid rope
Serving mallet or reel-type serving tool
Whipping twine
Sharp knife

Lay out your line forming the necessary eye. For the length of the splice, allow 7 or 8 times the inside width of the eye.

Place a tight seizing at the throat, then remove the tape or melted tip from the end of the tail and taper the tail smoothly with an angled cut through the coat and core. The cut should start 3 to 5 inches back from the end.

Comb, coax, and stroke the coat strands until they straighten along the axis of the tail. The strands will become indistinct, blending with the core yarns in the taper. Then "marl" down the tapered tail by firmly

Marling

binding it to the standing part with a series of hitches. Start at the beginning of the tail passing the twine through the heart of the standing part and putting a stopper knot in the end of the twine . Work away from the eye, to the end of the taper, tying off the other end in any convenient fashion.

Sew the two lengths of rope together between the marling and the seizing. Pass the needle and twine through the centers of both lengths of line by turns, pulling the twine as taut as possible as you go. Begin the stitching just below the throat seizing, and when you reach the marling start right back the other way, creating cross stitches as you go. Tie off the two ends at the throat with a Square Knot (see Chapter 13).

To set up the splice for serving, tie it up with a good strain, taut between two posts.

For serving, you will need a serving tool, which dispenses small stuff in tighter turns than you can possibly achieve otherwise, or a serving mallet, the traditional alternative.

Start the serving at the throat with twine and the mallet. After burying the end of the waxed twine beneath the first several turns, proceed with the serving until the entire splice is smoothly and tightly covered.

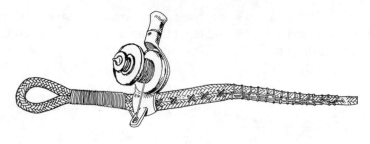

Service

Allow only the last 6 or 7 wraps to remain loose. Reeve the end of the twine back under the slack turns, snug the turns as tightly as possible, and cut the end close.

13

Quick and Easy Knots

The piecing together of rope and the placing of eyes, or loops, at the end of rope requires splices that offer a high degree of safety, strength, and dependability. The knots in this section, however, serve best in those light-duty situations not requiring the exceptional strength of a well-constructed splice. It is important to remember that the working load of a rope can be reduced by as much as half when it is knotted.

The Square Knot, or Reef Knot, is the most common. A Square Knot should not slip if it is tied with two ends of the same rope or two ropes of the same size, but it can lock under tension, making it difficult to untie. The Square Knot usually should not be used to join two pieces of rope. Tied wrong, this knot becomes a Granny Knot and more likely to slip.

The Package Knot is simply a Square Knot with an extra turn in the first overhand. It is a good alternative to the Square Knot because it is easier to untie. It does not hold as well, however.

The Bowline is a workhorse of a knot. There are many methods for tying it—all of them easy—and it's just as easy to untie. It's a good knot for forming a loop at the end of a rope.

A Bowline on a Bight is a good choice when you require two loops that will be subjected to approximately equal tension in the same direction. It works well as a bosun's chair.

The Fisherman's Knot is strong and easy to tie, but untying it is very difficult. (In the illustration, the knot has not yet been cinched tight.)

A bend is a knot used to join two lines. The Sheet Bend is much easier to untie than a Square Knot after it has been under strain, and is an excellent choice to join ropes of different sizes. When one of the ropes already has an eye in it, the knot is called a Becket Bend. It is important to pull the knot tight so the loops seat firmly with *like* ends parallel to each other. If this bend is not drawn tight properly, the two pieces can slip.

Towing hawsers can be joined with a Double Carrick Bend. If the ends are not seized onto the standing part of the rope, however, the knot can capsize under strain and be difficult to untie.

14

Making Your Own Rope

Rope designers use methods such as this when they work with a new fiber or yarn to get a feel for how much material is needed to make a specific rope and how much it will need to be twisted during manufacture. Many thousands of feet of rope have been sold from displays of short samples made this way.

TOOLS AND MATERIALS

Twine (at least 10 feet)
Scissors or sharp knife
Wooden pencil
Vinyl tape

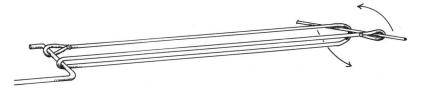

If you are using nylon twine, tape the ends to prevent unlaying. Tie one end of the twine to a fixed hook. Holding the pencil horizontally about 3 feet from the hook, alternately pass the twine around the pencil and hook until you have made at least 1½ complete rounds, the equivalent of three rope yarns. The diameter of the twine and the number of rope yarns formed will determine the diameter of the strand of rope you are making; this strand will be one half the diameter of the finished 3-strand rope, although you will triple your worked piece after the initial twisting.

When you have three or more yarns, tie off the unsecured end to the pencil or hook, and pull on the pencil to impose a uniform tension and length on the yarns.

Lightly grasp the bundle of yarns in the fist of your left hand with the pencil resting outside your thumb and forefinger. The tube formed by your fist is similar to a ropemaker's strand tube.

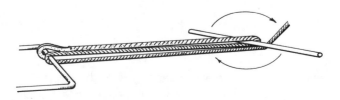

While keeping tension on the bundle of rope yarns with your fist, turn the pencil clockwise with the index finger of your right hand to form the rope strand. The number of twists you put into the strand will determine the firmness of the finished rope. You should stop twisting before the rope kinks, but if it does, just turn the pencil counterclockwise until the kink disappears.

Grasp the pencil with your right hand and keep tension on the strand throughout this step. With two fingers of your left hand grasp the strand midway between the pencil and the hook, forming a bight. Pass the pencil behind the hook and back again, inserting it through the bight of strand in your left hand. Don't let the strand go slack.

You now have three parallel and highly twisted strands. Grasp them with a fist as before, and twist the pencil counterclockwise until it stops. The finished rope will not unlay of its own accord. Ropemakers refer to this characteristic as "balance."

Tape the rope just shy of each end, and cut off the ends. You now should have a short piece of 3-strand rope that looks as though it was cut as a sample from a large spool of machine-made rope.

Glossary

Anchor cable. Chain, line, wire, or a combination of them used to attach a vessel to its anchor.

Belay. To secure a rope with turns around a cleat or bit.

Bend. Knot used to join two ropes.

Bight. A loop in a length of chain or rope.

Bitt. Wood or iron post on a deck for securing mooring or tow lines.

Bitter end. The nonworking end of a line or chain.

Bollard. Iron mooring post on a pier.

Breaking strength. Load required to break a rope under tension during a prescribed test.

Chafe. To wear or fray a rope.

Coat. Outer covering of two-part rope.

Coil. Neat circles of rope, line, or chain piled to keep the loops free of tangles.

Cordage. Rope or rope-like material varying in size from twine to hawser. In nautical handiwork, rope of less than ½ inch diameter, or small stuff.

Core. The inner section of two-part rope.

Diameter. Measurement of cross section of rope through the center. For noncritical use, determine by measuring rope's circumference, or girth, and divide by 3.

Eye. A spliced loop in a rope.

Fid. Tool used in splicing.

Halyard. Any rope or wire used to hoist sails.

Hardness. A measure of the force required to open the strand of a rope. A hard rope almost stands by itself.

Hawser. Towing or mooring line over 5 inches in circumference.

Hawsepipe. Metal tube that allows passage of the anchor cable to the chain locker.

Hitch. Knot used to tie a line to a hook, ring, or spar.

Hockle. A condition whereby a rope strand twists on itself. Also called a chinckle.

Jury Rig. Make or fix using ingenuity and whatever materials are at hand.

Kink. A tight hockle that upsets the lay of a rope.

Knot. A weak substitute for a splice, but easy to unfasten.

Lanyard. A length of small stuff, sometimes decorative, tied to an object to make it secure.

Lash. To secure with rope.

Lay. The direction of twist in a rope strand. (*See* Right-laid.)

Line. Rope with a specific use.

Make fast. To secure a rope.

Marl. A form of seizing.

Marline. 2-Strand, left-laid, tarred hemp.

Marlinspike. Steel tool used to separate strands in a wire rope during splicing.

Marry. To interlace two ropes, end-to-end, for splicing.

Mooring lines. Rope used to tie a boat to a wharf or pier.

Mousing. Seizing used to prevent a pin from unscrewing and falling out of the shackle or to close the opening of a hook.

Pic. Rib of a strand.

Preventer. A length of wire chain or line that acts as a safeguard or backup tether to keep an object (such as a boom) from moving unexpectedly.

Reeve. To pass the end of a rope through a hole.

Right-laid. Rope with strands twisted up and to the right when the end points away from the viewer.

Serving. A smooth covering on line or wire.

Serving mallet. Hammer-like tool used to apply wrapping turns around a line or splice.

Small stuff. Rope of less than ½ inch diameter.

Splice. Careful entwining of rope components.

Standing part. The area in the rope that is inactive, as opposed to the working end, bitter end, or bight.

Surge. Let the strain off a line intermittently, in a controlled fashion.

Tackle. A system of lines and blocks to gain additional lifting or pulling power.

Take a turn. Run a line around a cleat or bitts.

Taper. To diminish the diameter of a rope smoothly by selectively removing strands or yarns.

Thimble. A grooved ring made of plastic or metal that fits tightly inside an eye splice.

Twine. Bigger than a sewing thread, but smaller than a shoelace.

Unlay. Take a twist out of 3-strand rope to separate the strands.

Whip. Wrap the end of rope with small stuff to prevent the rope from unlaying.

Working load. A manufacturer's recommendation of the maximum pounds of pull that a rope can safely be subjected to; generally $\frac{1}{10}$ the new rope breaking strength.

Yarn. A group of fibers twisted together; thread.